"Visible G
Caleb's ins
fellow believers and navigate conflicts with a compassionate approach. It's a valuable resource that will undoubtedly benefit those seeking to deepen their understanding of grace and foster godly, grace-filled relationships within the church."

Greg Gilbert, Senior Pastor, Third Avenue Baptist Church, Louisville, KY

"In this book, Caleb Batchelor helps Christians love the local church by looking at the church through the lens of Jesus. When Jesus looks at His bride, He sees her beauty, her obedience, her service, her love for Him, even if imperfect. And yet, the reality is we often look out at our churches and focus on flaws and faults. Visible Grace comes in, then, and provides something of a spiritual LASIK surgery, correcting our view of Christ's people by pointing us to God's Word and the heart of Jesus. Read this book and (1) Repent of ways you've wrongly viewed the church; (2) Rejoice in what God has done and is doing in your church and other churches; and (3) Recommit to loving your church as Jesus does."

Omar Johnson, Pastor, Temple Hills Baptist Church, Temple Hills, MD

"When you think of your church, do you briefly glance at grace but stare at sin? Then this book is for you. Batchelor prescribes lenses to give us a God-like view of Christ's beloved community—the church."

J. Mack Stiles, Director, Messenger Ministries Inc. and author, *The Truth About Lies*

"The wonder of the Christian gospel is the grace extended toward sinners, toward the ungodly, toward God's enemies. When we experience God's grace and forgiveness, when we truly know that our only hope is found in God being merciful to us as sinners, then, as Caleb Batchelor reminds us in this book, we will see grace in the lives of others. We will seek to see grace in the life of the church. We will not be fundamentally critical or negative since we believe in a God who gives life to the dead, in a God who transforms us. Read this wonderful book to recall the grace of God in your own life and how you can be an agent of grace in the lives of others."

Dr. Tom Schreiner, The Southern Baptist Theological Seminary

"If you made a list of each person you criticized last week, and a list of each person you encouraged, which would be longer? Would your pastors and friends say you're more fluent in the language of criticism, or of encouragement? In an age of suspicion, biblical encouragement is a foreign tongue. It is rare currency—and thus deeply valuable. But it doesn't come naturally to self-absorbed sinners. This is why I'm grateful for Caleb Batchelor's timely book. It will help you to spy 'evidences of grace' in fellow believers, to become a fluent encourager, and to excel in the Bible's only competitive command: "outdo one another in showing honor". Read Visible Grace *and ask God to help you see and speak of others the way you hope they'll see and speak of you."*

Matt Smethurst, Lead Pastor, River City Baptist Church, Richmond, VA and author, *Before You Share Your Faith*

VISIBLE
GRACE

SEEING THE CHURCH
THE WAY JESUS DOES

CALEB BATCHELOR

10 Publishing
a division of 10 of those.com

British Library Cataloguing in Publication Data
A record for this book is available from the British Library

ISBN: 978-1-915705-47-1

Designed and typeset by Pete Barnsley (CreativeHoot.com)

Printed in Denmark

10Publishing, a division of 10ofthose.com
Unit C, Tomlinson Road, Leyland, PR25 2DY, England

Email: info@10ofthose.com
Website: www.10ofthose.com

1 3 5 7 10 8 6 4 2

CONTENTS

Introduction: Visible Grace 1

Visible Grace in Your Church 7

Visible Grace in Other Churches 17

Visible Grace in Disagreements 23

Visible Grace in Action 31

Conclusion: Visible Grace in Heaven 41

INTRODUCTION:

VISIBLE GRACE

I wouldn't follow myself on Instagram. Over the past few years, I've been posting pictures of my daughter at an exponential rate, and now I have two sons who are just brimming with social media potential. Yes, I'm one of *those* parents, and yes, I know it's ridiculous. I used to mock parents like me, but now I'm publicizing my kids' first words like they're the great pioneers of the English language—planting flags on the tallest linguistic summits. Like I said, it's a bit much. What happened to me?

Fatherhood. Kids came into my world, and a camera phone came out of my pocket. It just happened. Now, I notice every wonder about them, and I want everyone else to see too—kind of like another father I know.

Our heavenly Father celebrates every flicker of grace in his sons and daughters, and he invites the watching world to marvel with him (Matt. 5:16). He's poised, ready to take snapshots of grace in the church. And he doesn't need to strain his eyes to glimpse it. No, his grace is clear. It's conspicuous. It's visible.

How is that possible? Because God's grace is a reflection of himself.

What is grace? *Grace is the personal love of God for people who deserve the eternal wrath of God.* Because of our sin and God's holiness, we should be in hell right now, and what has God given us? His triune love (Rom. 6:23; Eph. 2:1–10; Tit. 3:3–7). The Father gave us his Son, love in the flesh, and through the Son, God—Father, Son, and Holy Spirit—offers us himself (Jn. 3:16; 16:7; 17:26). So, God's grace isn't impersonal, like tokens at an arcade or Skittles in a vending machine.[1] Again, grace is the personal love of

---

1   Michael Reeves, *Delighting in the Trinity: An Introduction to the Christian Faith* (Downers Grove: InterVarsity Press, 2012), p. 88.

God for people who deserve the eternal wrath of God. That's what God is looking at—or, perhaps, who he's looking at—when he looks for grace. He sees himself, the glorious, triune God, in the church (Eph. 3:20–21).

This is sometimes hard for me to believe.

I'm often more aware of my sin than God's grace, especially as the day progresses. I start the day with a fresh, white tee—looking good, feeling good—but by the end, after dribbles of doubt and spills of various sins, I look like I've been in a spiritual food fight. I'm not looking good or feeling good. And while Jesus loves me, surely he can't take his eyes off all the splotches? They're too distracting, too pervasive. That's what I think anyway.

Maybe you can relate. If Jesus had to describe you, what do you think would come out of his mouth first? Signs of his grace or your splotches of sin? While you may expect the latter, it would be the former: "if anyone is in Christ, he is a new creation. The old has passed away; behold, the new has come" (2 Cor. 5:17). Hallelujah! Dust off the church organ, grab a hymnbook, and "sing praises to God, sing praises" (Ps. 47:6)! Jesus can't think of you apart from the new creation you *are*. You may battle pride, doubt, or sexual sin, but your old self can't obstruct— try as it might—the grace in your new self. The Spirit's work is just too visible.

When Jesus looks for grace in your life, it's less like finding a needle in a haystack and more like spotting the sunrise in the dark sky. The smallest rays of grace escort sin into the background, each sunbeam from the Spirit stirring the heart of the Son. Perhaps you've shown humility with your co-worker! Or trust at the doctor's office! Or purity on social media! They're all visible to Jesus.

Unfortunately, apart from the Spirit, we don't naturally see the church the way Jesus does. Finding grace can feel like finding Waldo. We know grace is there—somewhere—but as hot tempers, cold relationships, infidelity, arrogance, grumpiness, bitterness, oppressive leadership, unremarkable sermons, lackluster programs, and unmet expectations fill the page, grace seems invisible.

Or, when grace does emerge, our gaze quickly returns to the sins of the saints.

If you had to describe your local church, what comes to mind first? Signs of God's grace? Or ways your church is falling short? I often assume the former but reflect on the latter. Michael's thoughtlessness catches my attention, Hannah's unreliability grates, and Jessie's impatience annoys me. Barely noticed are Michael's encouraging words, Hannah's care of elderly Christians, and Jessie's faithful presence at the Sunday morning gathering. I glance at grace and stare at sin.

Don't get me wrong. Looking for grace does not entail looking the other way when Christians sin (Gal. 6:1). And noticing sin does not necessarily make you a graceless curmudgeon. Until Jesus comes back, the church will sin. You'll see it, and you may need to confront it. Confession and repentance are fertilizers for growth, and we should till them into the soil of our churches (2 Cor. 7:9–10). But if we are seeing the church the way Jesus does, shouldn't grace be more remarkable than sin? I believe so, and that's what this little book is about.

1

VISIBLE GRACE
IN YOUR CHURCH

When friends and family visit, I like to take them to the Sandia Crest, a ridgeline overlooking Albuquerque, New Mexico. We'll also tour the city—hiking in the Pino Canyon or stopping for barbacoa tacos at El Paisa Taqueria—but from the Crest, you can see Albuquerque in one shot.

The Apostle Paul brought his friends to a similar overlook. Climbing the mount of Calvary, he walked the early church through the gospel, showcasing God's visible, expansive grace in their lives. And through his New Testament letters, Paul extends the same invitation to you.

If he had a membership directory of your church (a list of Christians in your church who have promised to care for each other), he'd flip through each page, pointing out God's grace in predestination, regeneration, justification, sanctification, and glorification.

Predestination: God has reserved your church

Paul didn't have access to a pre-released copy of the Book of Life. But that didn't shake his confidence that God "chose" the Thessalonians (1 Thes. 1:4). Paul didn't see Rufus' name printed on page 456 of heaven's guest list, but he wanted the Roman church to know that God "chose" Rufus (Rom. 16:13). What gave Paul license to make such bold claims? Because Paul knew grace doesn't come out of nowhere. Like rivers, grace comes from somewhere. So, when Paul saw a river of sanctification, he followed it upstream to the spring of predestination (Rom. 8:29–30).

After he heard about the Ephesians' faith in Christ and love for the saints, Paul thanked God for choosing them (Eph. 1:4–6, 15–16).

Faith and love: that was all Paul needed to hear before praising God for his predestining grace. He didn't wait until the Ephesians memorized Leviticus, and his prayer of thanksgiving wasn't limited to the most impressive church members. Paul wasn't looking for extraordinary resumes. He was just looking for signs of genuine conversion, and once he saw those, he sprinted to the predestining grace of God.

Friend, your church's membership directory is not the Book of Life, but if you're practicing regenerate church membership—receiving members who have made a credible profession of faith and repented of their sins—it's a pretty good rough draft. Look over *all* the names, not just the impressive ones. Do you see faith and love? If you do, praise God that he has reserved your church for himself.

Regeneration:
God has recreated your church

Years ago, my wife and I were members of a church that held a prayer meeting every Sunday evening. We noticed a pattern in how these dear friends began their prayers: "Father, thank you for saving [fill in the blank]." It didn't matter what the prayer request was. Someone might have asked for prayer for a sore throat, but inevitably, her salvation headlined the prayer.

Initially, I balked at these prayers. "Can't we come up with something more original? Why can't we just pray for her sore throat?" Over time, the Spirit showed me these prayers were not the problem. My heart was. I had grown cold to the miracle of conversion.

Not Paul. Regeneration wasn't boring to Paul. When he thought about the Ephesian church—made up of folks struggling to stay sober and kids memorizing yet another catechism—he pictured death, Satan, empty graves, and an eternal throne (Eph. 2:1–6; 5:18; 6:1–3). Is this how you think about your fellow church members?

Picture the faces you saw this past Sunday, or if you have one, pull your membership directory back out again. You're looking at folks who used to be dead, but now, they're alive. You're reading names of people who once were in darkness. Now, they walk in light (2 Cor. 4:6). God did this, and he deserves our worship. Praise him with the strings, pipe, and lute! Blow a trumpet! Clash some cymbals! And where's a tambourine when you need one (Ps. 150:3–5)!

Justification:
God has rectified your church

Paul didn't mince his words. When he wrote to the Roman church, he didn't ask them how their pets were doing. He talked about their "many trespasses" (Rom. 5:16). Most of us would be asking for a different pen pal. But Paul didn't end his sentence there. He brought up the Romans' many trespasses to highlight God's rectifying work of justification:

> And the free gift is not like the result of that one man's sin. For the judgment following one trespass brought condemnation, but the free gift following many trespasses brought justification (Rom. 5:16).

Friend, Jesus' righteousness covers every unrighteous thought, action, and practice of your church, and that reality should—it must— color your perception of the sins in your church. Although their sins are like scarlet, Jesus presents them as white as snow. Apart from the cross, they're red like crimson, but with the cross, they're white as wool (Is. 1:18).

My guess is that your prayer meetings are sparsely attended. But as you scan your church directory, the faithful zeal of Christ's prayers in Gethsemane covers the prayerlessness of Sam and Jason. Sarah seems to give in to temptation every four minutes, but Christ resisted for forty days in the wilderness on her behalf. Your church directory is full of sinners, but it's also soaked in the blood of Jesus. So, as you flip through its pages, make sin in the church a springboard to thank God for justifying the church.

Like many of you, I have drawn from Robert Murray McCheyne's encouragement to keep my eyes on Jesus: "For every look at yourself, take ten looks at Christ." But what if we applied this to our fellow church members' sins? What if, for every look at your church, you took ten looks at Christ?

Sanctification:
God is remaking your church

Fingernails changed the way I relate to other church members. Shortly after Leah and I found out we were expecting our first child, the doctor told us that our baby had fingernails. Earlier that fall, Leah wasn't even pregnant. But just a few months later, she was carrying a baby with fingernails, and I was changed forever. I couldn't care less about keratin, but those little proteins which formed my daughter's nails represented something greater, something glorious. They represented life.

So, when the doctor told us that my little girl had fingernails, here's what I didn't say: "But why can't she talk yet? When will she be able to do long division?" No, I just sat in the doctor's office with a silly grin on my face—struck by the reality that my daughter was growing, actually growing.

Friend, your brothers and sisters are still developing in Christ, just like my little girl was in her mother's womb. Don't expect every member, or even most, to be stalwarts of faith. They may not have a biblical view of x or y, but are they growing? If they are, the Father is smiling, and no one can wipe it off his face. He knows his children will continue to develop until they're full-term.

If the future development of believers was in question, it'd be difficult to rejoice in that little bit of growth. But it's not in question (Phil. 1:6). For those in Christ, their development is guaranteed, and since you can expect glorification, you can approach others' sanctification with "expectancy:" As Eugene Peterson writes, "A community of faith flourishes when we view each other with … expectancy, wondering what God will do today in this one, in that one." He continues, "It is impossible to be bored in such a community, impossible to feel alienated among such people."[2]

So, how is your church growing right now? Not, "How should they grow?" The latter's a great question to ask—a necessary question—but don't miss out on how God is remaking your church into his image right now. Give it some thought. Stop over each name in your directory and look for God's sanctifying grace. Look for the fingernails. And praise God for their growth!

---

2 Eugene Peterson, *A Long Obedience in the Same Direction: Discipleship in an Instant Society* (Downers Grove: InterVarsity Press, 1980), p. 176.

Glorification:
God will resurrect your church

The Colossians had a few milquetoast
members—folks who couldn't carry a
conversation or lead a Bible study. But Paul
knew what was coming (Col. 3:4). So, when
he prayed for them, he thanked his Father for
their imminent glorification (Col. 1:9, 12). The
Colossians' future resurrection transformed
Paul's present thankfulness.

If you're hoping that all your members
become evangelistic ninjas and exegetical
wizards tomorrow, I'm sorry to burst your
ecclesiological bubble but that's not happening.
In fact, they'll occasionally gripe and complain
when they tussle with the effects of the curse.

But glory's coming.

Living in Albuquerque, my family and
I like to swim in the Rio Grande. If I'm being
honest though, the Albuquerque portion
isn't impressive. It's small and, compared to
other sections, rather humdrum. But the Rio
Grande doesn't stop in Albuquerque. Starting in
Colorado, the 1,900-mile-long river dumps out

into the Gulf of Mexico. And the Gulf is not small. It's not humdrum.

As I look through our church directory and consider my own heart, we're in Albuquerque. We're not in the Gulf. But we will be. Because one thing is clear: rivers start somewhere, and they also end somewhere:

And those whom he predestined he also called, and those whom he called he also justified, and those whom he justified he also glorified (Rom. 8:30).

From the gospel mountain, you can see where salvation starts and where it ends in one shot—one beautiful, multi-faceted shot.

2

VISIBLE GRACE IN OTHER CHURCHES

Renew your passport. Hire a sherpa. We need to climb another mountain—the highest mountain. If chapter 1 was a view from the Sandia Crest, chapter 2 is a panoramic shot from Everest.

You have a standing invitation to witness beauty in your local church (chapter 1). But as we consider the Great Commission and the spread of gospel communities in the ancient world, the New Testament also takes us up into the Himalayas—showcasing God's visible, global grace in other churches (chapter 2). Do you see it?

When you think about churches in your city and around the world, what's your first impulse? Celebrating God's work in those churches? Or mulling over the ways they're "less healthy" than your church?

I've heard Mark Dever say, "The most important things about our church have to be the things that we have in common with every other true Christian church that there is in our city, country, or around the world—in all places, ever since Jesus."[3] Sadly, we often switch that around. We make our distinctives the most important things about us—over-emphasizing tertiary things, under-emphasizing the main things, and feeding a tribalistic tendency. How do we combat this?

There are many ways, but here's one: marvel at God's beauty in churches who are doing things "wrong."

That last word wasn't a typo. Thousands of churches are doing a million things you disagree with, and Jesus is caring for those churches

---

3   Mark Dever, "What All Healthy Churches Have in Common" (an article for Crossway's website, 2021); https://www.crossway.org/articles/what-all-healthy-churches-have-in-common/

in countless ways. As they lift his name up through their proclamation of the gospel, the Spirit of Christ is overcoming their apparent shortcomings out of his deep love for them and his divine power.

I'm not suggesting we minimize doctrinal precision or sound ministry philosophy. We should labor to be as biblical as possible. But let's also remember that Jesus isn't handicapped by the imperfections of other churches. And he's not handicapped by the flaws of your church. Your church is probably less healthy than you think, and God is undoubtedly using her more than you can imagine. Nothing can stop Jesus from loving his bride, the church, which means there's visible grace for us to witness.

Just think about all that will happen this week: new life through the preaching of the gospel; sacrificial love between members who don't share much in common except Jesus; and unknown pastors in unknown churches spending unknown hours in sermon prep, because God's Word is good, and his people need to hear it. God has created you to notice these manifestations of his grace. It's why he saved you (1 Pet. 2:9). Are you looking for them?

Are you looking for his grace in churches that are "more fruitful" than yours and in churches that are "less fruitful" than yours? Are you looking for his grace in churches that are "healthier" than yours and in churches that are "less healthy" than yours?

Union with Christ frees us to celebrate God's grace in gospel-preaching churches that span the range of fruitfulness and health. Since Jesus is our identity and their identity, we don't need to feel insecure about churches that are more fruitful and healthier. And we shouldn't feel superior to churches that are less fruitful and less healthy. Instead, we can feel deep gratitude for them because, in Christ, the grace you see in other churches is yours:

> So let no one boast in men. For all things are yours, whether Paul or Apollos or Cephas or the world or life or death or the present or the future—all are yours, and you are Christ's, and Christ is God's (1 Cor. 3:21–23).

Don't boast or cringe about your church. For all of God's grace in all his gospel-preaching churches—whether Presbyterian or

Pentecostal or Baptist or Anglican or Methodist or Sovereign Grace or Lutheran—all that grace is yours in Christ.[4] Name the church and claim the grace. Name it and claim it. Name the Presbyterian church on 4th street and claim their evangelistic zeal. Name the Pentecostal church in Tokyo and claim their faithfulness in prayer. Name the Baptist church in Cairo and claim their doctrinal integrity. Name the church and claim the grace!

You're a citizen of a diverse kingdom, a never-ending city of visible grace, and it's all yours. Every church is a new road that promises unique glory. Each congregation is a new peak with a landscape you've never seen before. And friend, it's all yours. Go. Explore. Discover.

---

4   Anthony Carter, "All Things Are Yours Interlude" in Shai Linne's album *Lyrical Theology*, "Part 1: Theology" (2013).

3

VISIBLE GRACE IN DISAGREEMENTS

What about disagreements? How can we enjoy the gospel views from the Sandia Crest or Mount Everest when Timmy is smacking his gum and Sally is blaring TikGram or InstaTok or whatever it's called? What happens when chapters 1 and 2 collide with differences and prickly sinners? Here are three things we should strive for:

1. Christians who are willing to confront but aren't eager for controversy.

2. Christians who pursue a gentle revival, not a holy war.

3. Christians who eavesdrop on Jesus' intercession instead of joining Satan's accusations.

Willingness to confront vs. eagerness for controversy

Paul wasn't afraid to address sin. Just ask the Corinthians. But what first grabbed Paul's attention when he thought about that rowdy, discriminatory congregation in Corinth? God's visible grace (1 Cor. 1:4–9). He was willing to confront, but he was not eager for controversy. There's a difference.

It's all about your posture. Do you find yourself on the edge of your seat, ready to engage in the latest controversy? Or is your preference to celebrate God's grace, ready to confront only when necessary (Prov. 15:18; 17:19)?

Jude had a preference:

Beloved, although I was very eager to write to you about our common salvation, I found it necessary to write appealing to you to contend

*for the faith that was once for all delivered to
the saints (Jude 3).*

He wanted to agree, celebrating God's grace
in their "common salvation." But he *needed* to
confront those "who pervert the grace of our
God into sensuality and deny our only Master
and Lord, Jesus Christ" (Jude 4).[5]

Like Jude, we shouldn't prefer controversy—
especially when it's simply to be entertained.

I feel contempt for those who attended the
gladiator games, where another's ruin was their
entertainment, where a father's wounds were
their source of glee. But then I remember a
talk I heard in middle school, where the speaker
compared our fascination with others' suffering
to the ancient appeal of the gladiator games.
It's convicting to think of how many times
I've laughed about another's sin, joked about a
pastor's blunder, and made sport of a church's
questionable ministry practice. As I scroll down
my Twitter feed, I descend the steps of a modern
coliseum, where another's moral ruin is my

---

5   Gavin Ortlund, *Finding the Right Hills to Die On*
    (Minneapolis: The Gospel Coalition, 2020), p. 94.

entertainment, where a father's spiritual wounds are my source of glee.

If you want to be countercultural today, don't let a pastor's moral failing or a stupid controversy fascinate you (1 Cor. 13:6; 2 Tim. 2:23). Pray. Grieve. Ask for grace. Confront when necessary. But don't feed your curiosity with others' sins. As the Puritan Richard Sibbes so helpfully points out:

> *"Men must not be too curious into prying into the weaknesses of others. We should labour rather to see what they have that is for eternity, to incline our heart to love them, than unto that weakness which the Spirit of God will in time consume."*[6]

Aren't you glad that Jesus feels burdened by your indwelling sin, rather than entertained by it? I'm thankful that my weaknesses elicit his warm compassion, not a witty Tweet.[7] Don't you want more of that heart toward your brothers and sisters in Christ? When they

---

6   Richard Sibbes, *Works*, 1:57.

7   Dane Ortlund, *Gentle and Lowly* (Wheaton: Crossway Books, 2020), pp. 69, 71.

disagree with you, do you "welcome [them] as Christ has welcomed you, for the glory of God" (Rom. 15:7; cf. Rom. 14:1–4)? When they walk in and everyone moves to the other side of the lunchroom, do you sit down next to them? When they don't deserve love, do you show them grace?

Since you have the Spirit of Christ, you already have that inclination. The Spirit of your gentle and lowly Savior abides in you. And the result is gentleness.

A gentle revival vs. a holy war

After Galatians 5:16–24, one of the most popular paragraphs on the Holy Spirit, what point does Paul double-click on? A gentle spirit:

> *If we live by the Spirit, let us also keep in step with the Spirit. Let us not become conceited, provoking one another, envying one another. Brothers, if anyone is caught in any transgression, you who are spiritual should restore him in a spirit of gentleness (Gal 5:25–6:1).*

That's weird. After a prolific treatise on the Spirit, doesn't denouncing provocation and encouraging gentleness seem like a strange place to go? It seemed odd to me. And then I read Jonathan Edward's report of the "Great Awakening." To describe one of the greatest revivals in church history, here's what he said,

> *When once the Spirit of God began to be so wonderfully poured out in a general way through the town, people had soon done with their quarrels, backbitings, and intermeddling with other men's matters.*[8]

That sounds a lot like Galatians 5:25–6:1 to me—an echo of the Spirit of Christ in Matthew 11:28–29.

Christian, one of the greatest evidences of the Spirit's work in a church is when she is marked by a spirit of gentleness. No, we can't budge on the gospel, and yes, we must contend for the faith (Gal. 1:6–9; Jude 3). But we'll never know the power of the Spirit apart

---

8   Jonathan Edwards, quoted in Iain Murray's book *Jonathan Edwards: A New Biography* (East Peoria: The Banner of Truth Trust, 1987), p. 115.

from the gentleness of the Spirit (Gal. 5:23; Eph. 4:29–32). So, we need to decide what we want more—a "holy war" or a revival? We must choose whether we'll be combative, jarring crusaders or courageous, gentle reformers. I'm praying that you want to be the latter. I'm praying for a revival.

The tone of Jesus' intercessions vs. the sound of Satan's accusations

Does the tone of your disagreements sound more like the intercessions of Jesus or the accusations of Satan?

While an antagonistic word can clearly communicate your position, doctrinal clarity is not a valid excuse to satanically accuse those for whom Jesus died (Rev. 12:10). It's never biblical to be diabolical to the unbiblical. So, when confronting a supposedly errant position, listen to Christ pleading his blood for the saint behind the position. Eavesdrop on the intercession of Jesus. Then reflect the posture of Jesus in your communication.

I wonder how our confrontations would change if we could hear Christ interceding in the next room?[9] If we heard him pleading,

Father, forgive them—They don't know what they're doing.
    Look at my righteousness—
    Don't look at their unrighteousness.

How would our tone change? How would our word choice change? Friend, let Christ's intercession for your brother or sister be the background noise as you confront them.

---

9   The idea of hearing Christ pray in the next room comes from Robert Murray McCheyne: "If I could hear Christ praying for me in the next room, I would not fear a million enemies" (*The Life and Remains, Letters, Lectures, and Poems of the Rev. Robert Murray McCheyne* [London: Forgotten Books, 2018], p. 138).

4

VISIBLE GRACE IN ACTION

To help us "be doers of the word, and not hearers only" (Jas. 1:22), here are eight practical ways to see the church the way Jesus does.

Commit to a church

I understand your hesitation. Committing to a local church *can* feel restrictive, like signing up for student loans. But it can also be liberating, like writing your name on a marriage covenant.

Married couples argue and disappoint each other, but in a climate of faithful, gracious commitment, they also notice qualities in their spouse that no one else does. They've traded their ideal spouse for a real one, and as they fulfill their promise to extend grace, true friendship flourishes.[10] The same principle applies to Christian community.

Idealized visions of the church destroy Christian community because they extract mercy from the bloodstream of Jesus' body and replace it with morality.[11] Like carbon monoxide, moralistic dreams of a quasi-glorified community de-oxygenate the church, leaving her gasping for mercy. They are deadly. But non-committal church attendance often inhales these fantasies—attending or not based on the likelihood of seeing an imaginary community realized.

True community operates differently. Joining a gospel-preaching church will suffocate your ecclesiological dreams, but your gospel blood cells will fill with mercy. You and your church

---

10 Tim Keller, *The Meaning of Marriage: Facing the Complexities of Commitment with the Wisdom of God* (New York: Riverhead Books, 2011).

11 Dietrich Bonhoeffer, *Life Together*, trans. John W. Doberstein (London: SCM Press, 1954), pp. 12–13.

will argue, disappoint each other, and destroy every dream of a perfect church, but you'll also notice grace in each other that no one else sees. You'll sin against one another, but you'll breathe deeply with one another.

Eat with your church

When conversation moves from the church parking lot to the dining room table, a shift happens, doesn't it? Pretense subsides. Dialogue deepens. Relationships blossom.

Don't underestimate the value of a lunch invitation, the power of a paper plate. If you want to see visible grace in your church, eat with your brothers and sisters in Christ. Before the Sunday morning gathering, make more gravy, buy an extra pie, and add a few more chairs around your table—for the easier members *and* the harder members.

In some ways, harder friendships make it easier to look for grace, because what else explains those friendships besides Jesus? If you don't vote like each other, dress like each other, joke like each other, or really do anything like each other except follow Jesus, what grounds your friendship? Not politics. Not style. Not humor.

Not anything or anyone else besides Jesus, who is the true foundation of Christian community. As Dietrich Bonhoeffer wrote, "One who wants more than what Christ has established does not want Christian brotherhood. He is looking for some extraordinary social experience … ."[12]

Hosting harder members probably won't feel like an "extraordinary social experience." Lunch may get awkward. But as you see Jesus in each other, it'll also be glorious, and God's grace will be the obvious centerpiece of your friendship.

Pray for your church

Billy Graham once said, "You cannot pray for someone and hate them at the same time." So, if you're struggling to see God's grace in other church members, pray for them.

Over the years, a practice I've found helpful is praying through my church's membership directory. Each morning, I write several one-sentence prayers based on my daily Bible reading. After praying for myself and my family members, I pray for my church, focusing each day on one letter of the church directory. Today, drawing

---

12 Dietrich Bonhoeffer, *Life Together*, p. 14.

from my reading of 2 Chronicles 7–8, I thanked the Lord that "everything needed for [all those with last names beginning with 'S'] to dwell in his house has been accomplished." Simple, right? It only took me a couple of minutes, but even a short prayer quickly reoriented my heart toward those members.

Text your church

When you think about how inconvenient letter writing was in Paul's day, the volume of encouraging letters he sent is astonishing. Just think about how many texts he'd send with unlimited data.

Why not message a fellow church member right now? Point out how you see God's visible grace in his or her life. Be specific. Perhaps share one of the prayers from your Bible reading. And "outdo one another in showing honor" (Rom. 12:10).

Gossip about your church and other churches

After you've texted church members, weave them into other conversations. I've heard Mark Dever refer to these edifying conversations as godly "gossip." The Apostle Paul sure did a lot of godly gossiping. He constantly talked about other churches behind their backs—speaking about God's work in those congregations. To the Thessalonians he wrote,

> *Therefore we ourselves boast about you in the churches of God for your steadfastness and faith in all your persecutions and in the afflictions that you are enduring (2 Thes. 1:4).*

When you have church members over for dinner, ask them, "Who at church has been an encouragement to you?" When new folks join your church ask, "What did you love about your last church?" And when other Christians come up in conversation, think about how you can speak well of them and showcase God's visible grace in their lives.

Connect with other churches

Most of us don't have the bandwidth to connect with other churches like Paul. I'm sure the Corinthians didn't have time to visit the Macedonians, but Paul still encouraged the Corinthian church to notice God's grace in the Macedonian churches (2 Cor. 8:1). And the Corinthians weren't the only ones to befriend other churches. The Macedonians reached out to the Thessalonians, who encouraged them in their walk with the Lord (1 Thes. 1:7). And the Thessalonians must have done some gospel networking themselves, because their "faith in God [went] forth everywhere" (1 Thes. 1:8).

How can we also connect with churches in our city and around the world? Here are three ideas:

1. *Pray* for other churches. Ask friends at other churches how they're encouraged about what God is doing in their churches, and then praise God for his grace to your friends.

2. *Recommend* other churches. If members live closer to a like-minded, gospel-preaching congregation, maybe you should recommend that church to them. Recommending other churches shines the light on God's grace, not on us.

3. *Visit* other churches. When you travel, worship with another church instead of spending that time on the road.

Visiting other churches can be mutually encouraging as you celebrate what God is doing in each other's lives (Rom. 1:11–12).

Disagree infrequently

When I'm regularly spotting the wrong in others, there's a good chance I'm trying to distract myself from all that's wrong in me. If I can reflect on how I'm right and another person or group is wrong, it helps me forget about my own insecurities. It's a sober way to quiet my inward turmoil.

A judgmental heart inebriates a condemned conscience. It makes us forget about our sin for a moment. But as we're well aware, passing judgment can't take care of our sin for eternity. After the intoxicating effects of judging others have worn off, the pain of our sin washes over us yet again. So, what do we do? We become "judge-aholics." We stock our minds with enough disagreements to block out our insecurities, self-medicating our anxiety with weaknesses in the church. But as we empty shot glass after shot glass of doctrinal spats and squabbles, we can't see God's visible grace.

So, if you see yourself disagreeing often, here's a mental checklist to work through: rehearse who you are in Christ *first*, see God's grace in others *second*, and then disagree *third*. You may find yourself disagreeing just as much, but I doubt it.

Disagree occasionally

Over the past couple of years, a good friend and I have disagreed on several important issues. We're not debating about whether Chick-fil-A or Popeyes has the better chicken sandwich (Popeyes is better by the way). We're considering weighty, society-shaping issues. What I found intriguing though—perhaps more than the debates—is that we've left these conversations with greater unity. How does that work? I only have one explanation: Jesus.

Disagreements can disseminate a heavy fog, decreasing the visibility of grace in each other, but when we lift up the Son in our differences, his light evaporates the droplets of dissent and showcases his visible grace.

Debate affords you the opportunity to see this phenomenon unfold. So, disagree—not frequently, but occasionally.

CONCLUSION:

VISIBLE GRACE IN HEAVEN

Don't let the splotches on earth keep you from seeing the spotless church in heaven (Eph. 5:27). Don't stop looking for grace in the wrinkles. You'll see grace without wrinkles soon enough. The time will come when we'll turn to each other and say,

> *"Let us rejoice and exult*
> *and give him the glory,*
> *for the marriage of the Lamb has come,*
> *and his Bride has made herself ready;*

it was granted her to clothe herself
*   with fine linen, bright and pure"—*
for the fine linen is the righteous
deeds of the saints.
(Rev. 19:7–8)

On that day, looking for grace in the church won't be a challenge anymore, because God's grace in the church will be visible everywhere—visible forever.